'You'll Never Beat a 1500'

BY R

S o said Arthur Weavers, our chief locomotive inspector at Stratford in t
he was, of course, being provocative as we had not only some splendid   ...en if
they were referred to as 'Bleedin' old Bongos') but also the 7MTs which were the
best engines Stratford had ever had for the fastest and, at times, heaviest work. But Arthur
had fired on both the original B12s and the rebuilt B12/3s and he had, I believe, reached
the '1500 gang' as a driver before being appointed inspector. The drivers at that time in
the 1500 gang would be about 50, maybe less, and the older men in the top links worked
the very intensive steam-hauled suburban services which demanded not only experienced
men but great skill particularly in the use of the Westinghouse brake. But the 1500 gang
retained its name years into the diesel era, probably until many of the staff had been
transferred to a new Liverpool Street signing on point as part of the ultimate closure of
Stratford Depot.

Parkeston Quay was a remarkable little shed next door to Harwich and Dovercourt
which had always worked the 'Hook of Holland Continental' leaving Liverpool Street at
8pm. The load was getting bigger and bigger and the schedule tighter and tighter through
1920 until 1927 when new stock raised the weight to 459 tons and the schedule which for
some years had been 82 minutes for the 69 miles in the Down direction was eased to 87
minutes. For a 1500 in its original condition this meant very hard work.

There were four sets of men in the link who, in their different ways, were quite
outstanding as they had to be for a 1500 hauling a 415-ton train on so tight a schedule
over quite a heavy road. How was it done way back in 1922? Well, Cecil J Allen travelled
on 1566 with driver Harry Chapman and fireman Augustus Dale and, thanks to him
and his monthly offering in *The Railway Magazine*, we can see how it was done. In the
paraphrased words of CJA, 'This is one of the finest runs I have ever timed on the Down
'Hook Continental' with driver Chapman at the regulator of 1566 and a load of 13 bogies,
including two Pullmans and restaurant cars, 388 tons tare and 415 tons loaded. Fireman

Ipswich-based 61562, yet to
receive its smokebox number
plate, heads the 10.40am
Gorleston to Liverpool
Street train near New Hall,
Chelmsford on 6 August 1949.
LCGB KEN NUNN COLLECTION

Dale had his fire in first-class order for starting – so much so that when we were held for a minute waiting for a laggard empty coach train to get clear into no. 8, the fury of the steam blowing off sounded sufficient to lift off its bedplates the Pindar Street bridge under which we were standing! Soon we were up and over the top at Bethnal Green and through Stratford in less than eight minutes and then roared – literally roared – through the eastern suburbs. With 40 per cent cut-off and wide-open regulator, the engine accelerated to a steady 55mph up the gradually rising gradients to beyond Harold Wood and we were going magnificently up Brentwood Bank proper when the Yard distant was seen to be on and there was a perceptible drop in speed until the home and starter were pulled off. Chapman advanced his cut-off first to 50 per cent and finally to 60 per cent with full regulator and, to the accompaniment of a thunderous exhaust echoing from cuttings and woods, we climbed the final 1 in 77/90 at a steady 33mph, the boiler of 1566 finding ample steam for every demand made on it.' And so said Cecil J Allen way back in 1922. They were past Shenfield in under 28 minutes and Chelmsford in 36½, running into Parkeston Quay in 80 minutes for the 69 miles. Quite marvellous and repeated in future articles time and again. No wonder when Augustus Dale came to see me at Stratford on his retirement in 1956, he spoke of old 'Rocky' Chapman with affection and respect although he did make the point that he used to run the Hook engine with an enormous fire, constantly replenished until they were past Shenfield when things could be taken a little easier. On the other hand, Albert Sadler of a later generation (he had 1226 in the B1 link) told me that after Rocky had arrived on the shed, left the engine and booked off duty, nobody would go near the smokebox until it had cooled down hours later, for it was full of ash up to the top of the blast-pipe, right back to the tube-plate and red hot at that!

> **" Chapman advanced his cut-off first to 50 per cent and finally to 60 per cent with full regulator to the accompaniment of a thunderous exhaust ... "**

Before I make a comparison with the rebuilt B12/3, let Frank Cocksedge of Ipswich have a word. He had been one of the firemen on 8561 before the Manchester lodge link was formed in 1927 when his mate Jack Pack moved up. For years after I left Ipswich we corresponded and, referring to the B12s, he put it in a nutshell. 'How glad I am of one thing and it's just this: that I knew and worked on those engines in their prime. And what work it was too: Yarmouth, Norwich, London, the 3.30pm Down with 15 bogies, the "Antwerp Continental" and – the highlight of it all – an emigrant special from here to Liverpool Central, firing to Jack Pack on our own 8561, 13 bogies unassisted from Sheffield to Dunford and that on one fire, no chance to clean it. Ah, I think one can say it was a case of a good engine, a good mate and good work. I remember when there was a speed up and those engines were doing magnificent work. The attack on Brentwood bank, I can hear them now and how thrilled I was to be engaged in it. I think I can safely say that in many respects, "those were the days" and I have done my best to infuse something of that spirit into my mates and I feel that I have not entirely failed either.'

Classified S69 by the Great Eastern Railway, the first five 1500s were turned out of Stratford Works in 1911–12, another 15 in 1913 and a further 21 between 1914–17. After the war, in 1920–21, Messrs Beardmore supplied a further 20 and Stratford Works a final ten which takes us to 1570. But this was not the end for, in 1928, H N Gresley gave Beyer Peacock an order for ten more engines, 8571–8580, slightly altered in detail appearance and with Lentz oscillating cam valve gear. It is worth noting that 1500–1549 were fitted with Stone's adjustable blastpipe which were not removed until after the grouping but you can bet your boots that old 'Rocky' was using some form of artificial respiration in the blastpipe of 1566 on that memorable night in 1922. The 2800 B17 class started to come to the GE section in 1929 and between 1931 and 1943, a further 24 unrebuilt B12s were transferred to the Great North of Scotland section. They took over much of the heavier work and earned great popularity despite that long route march between the tender and the firehole door so frequently referred to in books and articles but no handicap to a strong, fit fireman such as Willie Alexander who later came from Kittybrewster to Carlisle and who remembered with great pleasure those splendid old B12s.

The Lentz engines were not an unqualified success although they moved fast with a lovely rhythm nor did they pound in the axle-boxes nor pull the water down against the exhaust injector when working hard. Wilfred Brown, chargeman fitter in my day at Ipswich and a splendid craftsman like so many of the artisan staff at Ipswich, was selected to be the Lentz specialist on 8577. He dedicated his skill to the perfection of this engine which was nominated to the irascible driver 'Sweater' English, the supreme coal dodger who was said to have got 8577 down to 25lbs of coal a mile on heavy work. So he may have done but 8577 was timed by CJA on one occasion as 'having made a desperately slow start from Ipswich passing Belstead summit at 19 mph!' Serious faults (which did not seem to assail 8577) soon developed with twisted camshafts and cracked cylinder castings and a decision was taken to replace the Lentz valves with normal piston valve distribution. Six of the older B12s had also been fitted with the Lentz gear and all were converted by January 1934. The last six to be built, 8575–80, were the first to be converted to class B12/3 with long lap, long travel valves and larger boilers, starting with 8579 in May 1932.

Before we look at the rebuilt engines that I knew so well and admired so much, let 1561E have the last word from Copley Hill, Leeds of all places, for she was based there from April 1924 to February 1925 after which she went home to Ipswich whence she had come after a short spell at Doncaster. I would never have known this had it not been for a Copley Hill fireman who had started there on 31 December 1922 and who used to say, with some pride, that he was a GN man. I thought a great deal of the Great Central B4 class of which 6100 was still at Copley Hill for the heavy 'Mail' to Doncaster after years of hard work before the war over the West Riding and to Grantham as well as 'specialling' to London, the East Coast resorts and over the Pennines to points west. But Stan Hodgson used to pull my leg about those old Imminghams. 'Dirty, coal-scoffing old "Poggies", we had an engine when I was a young fireman, a Sweedy engine, six wheel coupled that would run the "Poggies" silly.' What its class was Stan neither knew nor cared but said that she was a marvellous engine with a huge cab that needed a double shuffle from tender to firehole and rode like a coach. I asked him what the number was and after a lot of thought he replied, '1561E and she was a clipper, Dick'.

This photograph was taken from (the driver's side of) the cab of 61572 on the slow line and is believed to be the approach to Stevenage station.
DAVID BUTCHER

In 1956, inspector Arthur Heaton of Ardsley came south to Stratford for a Southend punctuality drive. So he rode on the rebuilt 1500s all the week with as much pleasure as he had experienced on that perfect day out in 1924 when he fired 1561E from Leeds to Wembley on a football special. Arthur said to me that he loved firing that engine and 'the best of those you have now are even better'. No doubt Arthur Weavers had already said to him, 'Arthur, you can keep your bloody GNers and you'll never beat a 1500'. And now for those rebuilt B12s of very happy memory.

By the time the B17s began to arrive it was clear that the B12s were having a tough time and that something stronger and more economical was needed to supplement the B17s on the heaviest work. After some experimental work on 8559, that remarkable triumvirate of Messrs E Thompson, Mechanical Engineer, Stratford, A. English, his Technical Assistant and the Locomotive Running Superintendent, L P Parker, got to work on a design which included a larger boiler with round-topped firebox as well as completely redesigned cylinders, valves and valve gear. The boiler was now 5ft 6ins in diameter and the new and larger firebox 31sq ft against 26½ sq ft of the original engines which also had a shallow level grate at the back-end but then sloped downwards towards the tubeplate. The superheater heating surface was markedly increased but the boiler pressure remained the same at 180psi. The alterations sent the weight up to 69½ tons against 63 tons of the originals, but by increasing the weight on the bogie that on the coupled wheels was within the GE Section maximum axle load of 17 tons.

Although the same cylinder and steam chest castings were used, the valve gear was completely redesigned. The new 'marine' expansion links had longer slots and shorter expansion links with an increase of the angle of advance of the eccentrics. When the new gear was pulled up to 15 per cent the maximum opening to exhaust equalled the full width of the ports. A number of detailed alterations were made – the air-reversing gear was removed, as were the GE pattern snifting valves, whereas the frames and the unusual setting for an inside cylindered engine of the coupling rod pins at the same angle as the

cranks remained as, of course, did the Westinghouse brake on engine and tender. Despite the changes in appearance, the rebuild was so obviously Stratford design and, as far as I know, no alterations were made by the Doncaster drawing office or by Gresley's technical staff to the Thompson/English inspired drawings. As I have frequently said, ET was responsible for much good work during his time as CME. Bert Spencer was well known as Gresley's technical man – a very different type to the abrasive, indeed waspish, but equally able Albert English – who expressed to me his high opinion of Thompson's work in general. As for the man who was to be my chief from 1945 to 1952, he was in a class of his own. So let us remember with gratitude these three engineers for their achievements in creating a remarkable flying machine with a sharp clear exhaust and the ability to run at the short cut-offs with the wide-open regulator so beloved of L P Parker.

The rebuilds were not only faster but more economical and they retained the lovely ride of the original engine. The cab was very comfortable with a shorter distance between tender and firebox door. But – and there must always be a 'but' – that level shallow grate at the back end presented a problem to a fireman if coal built up at the point where the slope began and formed a hump which prevented further charges reaching the front of the long firebox. A good fireman will run with plenty under the door and then make sure that his firing reaches the front and the built up back will help him with his swing so that the coal goes sailing past the point where the level grate ends.

Certainly the original engines had their mechanical faults, which is not to be wondered at, but the rebuilds had to be watched and regular manning of locomotives worked wonders for the enginemen. But at a place like Ipswich there was also a close understanding between the chargehand fitter and chargehand boilermaker, both the sons of Ipswich drivers and both men of the highest quality on the one hand, and on the other hand the enginemen keen to keep their charges at the top of the tree. What a joy this was for a shedmaster and at Ipswich I did everything that I could to encourage this understanding. A 1500 driver would call on Jack Percy and tell him that 'the valves on my old gal are beginning to blow

1566 and 1561, together with 1570, in their rebuilt days at Ipswich shed. The locomotives have full tenders but wait cleaning prior to working afternoon trains to London c1951.
DR I C ALLEN/ TRANSPORTTREASURY.CO.UK

through a bit, can you have her in, Jack?' The engine might only have run about 15,000 miles since the valves had last been done and they were supposed to do 30,000–36,000 miles between full valve and piston examinations, so Jack could easily have said that it was far too early to do the job. But he knows the engine intimately, is almost sure what is wrong, and he knows the drivers, who have both had something to say, are not wafflers – so the job gets done and everybody is happy. The same goes for small and big ends which, on the B12/3s, would rarely if ever reach the mileages laid down so if a small end started to knock, the driver knew that before long the big-end would follow suit and then run hot. Jack would be informed and the engine stopped as soon as possible for the work to be done which for an experienced Ipswich fitter dealing with a well-maintained machine was child's play. And it was the same with Charlie Winney, right at the top as a chargehand boilermaker, for any problems with any engine were closely watched and then everything dealt with at the double. The B12 boiler gave no trouble to Charlie although the best boiler of all, in his opinion, was the 100A Thompson boiler on the B1s and on some of the B17s. For all that, the B12s in the Stratford district where maintenance was carried out under great difficulties did not always respond too well although there again at Southend the regular manning of the B12s such as 1571, 1573 and 1575 helped enormously to keep the engines in as good condition as possible.

Before moving on to Ipswich, where we had eight B12s all in excellent condition, I must not forget that in April 1948, 1545 was transferred to Yarmouth Beach and was booked on a diagram that included the eastbound 'Leicester' from South Lynn. She was an immediate success but, sadly, we were sent the old K2s for our new through workings in June 1948 because the new diagrams (which were largely my work) included freight work such as the Yarmouth 'Fish' through to Peterborough. Had it not been for this, the odds would have been on us having B12s and I doubt if it is generally known that late on in 1948, maybe early 1949, chief inspector Len Theobald of Mr Parker's headquarters and I carried out a trial with a B12 on the 'Fish' with a full load and she ate the job. We got to Peterborough with plenty of time to get down to East station and catch the 'Mail' to March where we spent the night in the Barracks near the station. Not long after I had left South Lynn in June 1948, the regular manning of the old 'Ragtimers' was abandoned and when one or two B12s came to South Lynn and worked the hardest passenger jobs, the elderly gentry in the Passenger gang could do their work in comfort once more, although there were never enough to bring in regular manning again. Syd Cox said in a letter written to me after he retired that 'the old "Raggies" never killed me but now you can pension me off with a 1500 anytime'.

And so to Ipswich where we had two main line passenger links, B1 and B12. The B12s normally worked to Yarmouth South Town, London, Norwich and Cambridge and there were seven engines and 14 sets of men. Our engines were 1535, 1561/2, 1564, 1566, 1569 and 1570, all double manned and all with scoured up footplates where everything that could be polished shone like the sun. The drivers and engines in 1950–51 were nominated as follows:

- 1535 Jim Calver and Charlie Parr;
- 1561 George Dennant and Archie Rowe;
- 1562 Percy Burrows and Ernie Dunnett;
- 1564 Alf Alderton and Ted Bishop;
- 1566 Fred Thorpe and Maury Hood;
- 1569 Frank Cocksedge and Jock Coleman; and
- 1570 Fred Gibbs and Vic Trenter.

1577 was a spare engine. If more cover was required, our B17s, some of which had 225psi boilers, were common user engines and would replace B1s as well as B12s. Every evening I satisfied myself that, wherever possible, each driver had his own engine next day and right to the end and long into retirement, our men would talk of 'my old gal' with a pride which had been cultivated by those in charge. Deep in my own retirement, I was invited to the annual ASLEF evening at Ipswich and after the dinner and speeches, I went the rounds and there was driver George Dennant, very old by this time and not in good form nor easy to talk to. But when I mentioned his 1561, his eyes lit up. 'Gaw', he said, 'my old gal, 1561, she went off the boil and you came and rode with us as far as Colchester and she wouldn't boil nor run so you had her in and old Jack Percy, he ran the rule over her and found out what was wrong and a few days later, we had her again on the 7 o'clock up and you came

Ipswich Loco running shed in all the glory of its two roads. It is a Sunday morning late in 1951 and 'old thuty-five' (as Charlie Parr would call his beloved engine) has been washed out and lit up for an evening London job and maybe down with the Norwich 'Mail'. She will be polished and thoroughly gone over by the young cleaner-boys and she will look good although the paintwork was rough and unlined but polished steel and brass make a world of difference. I have a 1952 seniority list and I think the smart young lad is E Rayner, who started in August 1950 and the one on the right is F Sturgeon but I may be wrong – and would love to be factually corrected. Certainly on the left is Tammy Gooch the chargehand cleaner, an ex-engineman who died suddenly less than a year later. He would be working with the boys to make up the usual gang of four cleaners to an engine. Note the size of the pit on the right and it will be duplicated under 1535. It is fascinating to think that this picture was taken 60 years ago – the little lads will be in their middle 70s and yet it seems to me like yesterday.
DR I C ALLEN/TRANSPORTTREASURY.CO.UK

with us to Colchester and she was as good as gold, the old gal.' So it was my pleasure to do everything I could to nurture that pride in the job.

Let us think of 'old thuty five' as her driver used to call her – 1535 and driver Charlie Parr. One evening I had been talking to the running foreman on duty, Bill Thurlow, who had done some of his main line firing at Parkeston. He told me about his engine having a cream coloured 'hood', the inside of the cab roof which on a B12 in those days was wooden. Next day, I had to go to Diss and on my return caught the Ipswich all stations which ran in with 1535 and Charlie's opposite mate, Jim Calver. What a sight for sore eyes was that cab with everything burnished and shining, even the air-operated water scoop gear on the tender and when not otherwise engaged as we went along both men were doing a bit here and there, anything to make her sparkle. It occurred to me to ask Jim whether he would like her hood painted cream and the rest of the cab maybe chocolate colour. 'Gaw, why not, we'd make her shine', and so she did with the roof tallowed every day and after dark it shone and gleamed in the firelight. A few days later, there was a knock on my door and in comes driver Fred Thorpe of 1566, chairman of the Local Departmental Committee, and a very direct and blunt spoken man, sometimes fiery but as straight as a ramrod. 'What's this I hear about Calver's bloody engine all painted up in the cab, what's wrong with my old nag, why can't we have one?' 'Of course you can, Fred, next time she's shed.' 'Oh', says Fred taken aback for once in his life, 'that'll do then, good day'. So Fred and Maury Hood had a cream cab to knob up amongst other things. What a waste of time and money you might say but you would be wrong for our budgets were punctuality, pride in the job, cleanliness and good order and fair but firm discipline and self-discipline, a few of the things that really mattered in those days.

The time was when E S Cox, responsible for the design of the BR standard fleet, decided to come down to Ipswich on 70000 *Britannia* on 'The Norfolkman', then 10.00am from Liverpool Street, on her second day's work at Stratford. We had been told that he would be riding back to London on the engine of the 2.15pm Ipswich to Liverpool Street and 1535 was the booked locomotive for the job with driver Jim Calver, fireman Eddie Simpson and joined by chief inspector Len Theobald who had come down with Mr Cox on 70000. 1535 looked a picture despite her rough black paint devoid of lining and we were going to show a mere 'Midland' man what we could do and do it for L P Parker whom we knew, through Len, would be waiting at the buffer stops in London. Jim had the throttle wide open where it was needed and the gear often up to 15–20 per cent cut-off, coasted silently with the gear at 15 per cent, a lovely touch with the brake. His mate, Eddie, kept the steam a fraction below the red mark all the way, never blew off steam, never made heavy smoke, swept up after every firing, kept the dust down without spattering ESC's polished shoes, called all the signals and fired to the 'distants'. The job was done just so and LPP was at the buffer stops in his bowler and wash leather gloves to welcome E S Cox back after 1535 had come silently up the platform and to a perfect halt short of the buffer stops.

As for old Charlie Parr, he lived just outside the gate and when he was on the 'Mail' Down at 22.30 and Up with the 18.00, he would have his pint and then walk to the shed to be sure that he had got 1535 booked to him after wash-out, the normal practice. Having stumped along with his little pipe smoking away, he would ask, 'have I got old '35 tonight, foreman?' 'Yes, Charlie, she's been washed out and she'll soon be in steam.' So off Charlie would go, pipe on, a happy man. But one day, the laconic but humorous running foreman Bob Fenning was on duty when Charlie arrived and posed the usual question. Bob replied with a dead-pan face, 'Sorry, Charlie, the Cockneys pinched your old engine up in London last night and you've got a Stratford 'Ragtimer' tonight, they tell me you might get old '35 on the 'Mail' Down, if you're lucky'. Charlie's face went very grey, his pipe went out and he flew into such a rage that Bob had to intervene. 'It's alright, Charlie, don't worry, go and have your dinner, she's been washed out and lit up and she's over on the "Back Hadleigh", she'll be all ready for when you come on this evening.' 'That'll do then, foreman' says Charlie, magically happy again and he stumps off home no doubt to give his wife the story in every embellished detail.

It is well known that the rebuilt B12s did a good job on the ambulance trains during the war when they were stationed in the West Country at both GW and SR sheds. They

61576, complete with 'Invicta' Railway Correspondence and Travel Society headboard, at Stratford prior to hauling RCTS 'Hertfordshire Rail Tour' special on 30 April 1955. The B12 was one of four locomotives used, its leg took the tour from St Pancras to Hatfield via Kentish Town, Junction Road, Upper Holloway, South Tottenham, Northumberland Park, Brimsdown, Cheshunt, Broxbourne, St Margarets, Ware, Hertford East, Hertford Goods (old station), Hertford North, Cole Green and Welwyn Garden City. The tour proceeded to St Albans, and visited Watford, Rickmansworth, back to Watford and on to St Pancras sidings then King's Cross and Finsbury Park.
R E VINCENT/
TRANSPORTTREASURY.CO.UK

had GE crews, working 12-hour shifts, two sets of enginemen and a fitter to each train, ready for duty at a moment's notice – and all volunteers. The trains were Westinghouse-fitted and, with their light axle-load, the 1500 could go everywhere that mattered. A great comradeship developed between the railwaymen and the American servicemen who manned the trains and the only time there were words was when an assistant engine was required to hump the train over the most severe gradients. The leading driver took charge of the brake which, on a GW engine, was vacuum fitted and would operate the Westinghouse brake on the 1500 and on the train through the latter's proportional valve. And then came trouble for if the GW man was at all heavy-handed with his vacuum application it would be transmitted through the B12 to the very much sharper 'Westo' brake on the train with a series of violent jerks resulting in an equally sharp reaction from the American surgeons and doctors. So the GE men (who always had a GW pilot-man) usually prevailed upon the chap in front to keep his hands in his pockets! The 1500s were respected on both the Southern and GW (which is saying something) and the GE men, particularly the Cockneys, like the comical and brass-voiced Syd Cook of Stratford, were great ambassadors and gave the Americans endless amusement and happy memories to take home after the war.

Maybe there is space for two final experiences with 1576 of Southend and 1566 of Ipswich, the former in excellent condition having recently had a general repair and the latter in a pretty rough condition, sometime late on in 1957. When we changed over to 1,500dc electrification on the Southend road over the last weekend of 1956, the Saturday was going well and as assistant District Motive Power Superintendent at Stratford, I was well satisfied and in the mood to travel back to London on 1576 working the 9.34pm Up, the last steam-hauled train that day. The driver was passed fireman Ron Meeson, still in good form and who had fired 1571 for some years before getting passed for driving. We were all stations to Shenfield and having done very well to Wickford, Ron gave her the whip and we roared up Billericay bank at 1 in 100 at a steady 50mph with our packed eight coach set. I fired to Ron who said there was a solid column of fire going up the chimney but the engine steamed perfectly, held her water up and blew off when Ron shut off for Billericay before I had time to put on the second injector. At Shenfield we changed over and I had hold to Stratford so we had a nice little sprint over Ingrave summit and down towards London. It was an unforgettable evening which Ron and I have never forgotten for we were two youngish men with the adrenaline flowing but we knew exactly what we were doing. As for the Sunday on the final scheduled steam passenger working, before the electrics took over on the Monday morning, have you ever scored a century one day and been out for nought first ball the next? I'll leave it at that.

> **"I fired to Ron who said there was a solid column of fire going up the chimney"**

Before the railtour 61576 was sent down 6 Road in the New Shed (1871 construction) and was given the Stratford Running Shed treatment. Roy Vincent, who took three photographs, decided to photograph the '6 Road' men who did the job. The men in the cab are fireman John Day (between the uprights) and driver John Jackson. On the ground, left to right, are driver Harry Hollick (on light work who had supervised the cleaners), acting inspector Percy Howard, fitter Bill Patmore, his assistant Vic Burrows, Les Clarke (a fitter who had met with a serious accident and was still on light work), Alex Alexander, fitter Cyril Smewin, fitters mates Ray Langstaff and Ron Jessop, machinist Ron Bradley and mechanical foreman Arthur Day.
R E VINCENT/
TRANSPORTTREASURY.CO.UK

R H N Hardy and some of the Stratford shed and District management team. Although we worked together as a team, Stratford shed and District offices together, both District Motive Power Superintendent (DMPS) and Assistant District Motive Power Superintendent (ADMPS) played our part in running Stratford shed working closely with Dick Robson, Shedmaster. Left to right: Harold Davis, Chief Clerk to DMPS; Dick Robson, Shedmaster; Arthur Day, Mechanical Foreman; Bert Hurst (front) and Clive Dunkley, RCTS; Les Thorn, Technical Assistant; R H N Hardy, ADMPS Stratford; and Charlie Smith, Chief Running Foreman.
R E VINCENT/
TRANSPORTTREASURY.CO.UK

And my last journey on a B12 in regular service was just as memorable. John Greenfield of Stewarts Lane, a dedicated railwayman who had been our punctuality clerk in my time at Battersea, was keen to travel on a 1500 before it was too late so I asked Ipswich if they could put a B12 on the 8.01pm Up, a sharply timed train, Manningtree, Colchester, Witham, Chelmsford and fast to London. Our driver, who was delighted to have a 1500 for a change instead of a B1 or a diesel, was a very droll character who had 1561 in my time at Ipswich and was now the senior driver in what was left of the B1 link, a certain Archie Rowe. He was a broad-spoken Suffolk countryman, known to all as 'Speed the Plough'. He came to work from Chelmondiston on an elderly but completely reliable motorbike, wearing an old cloth cap, a fawn mackintosh, overalls and bike clips. He was never in trouble, was an excellent engineman and always the same, never got excited, a splendid mate. He knew that 1566 was now a bag of bones, dirty, rough, her wedges were down, she knocked in her axleboxes and her big ends too whilst her side rods scraunched in agony on curves but she would go and she would steam, my goodness yes. At Manningtree, Archie suggested to his mate, Peter Parsey I think, that he might be more comfortable in the train which left me to do the work, not hard with Archie driving. For all that, we burned a fair amount of coal at the front of that long firebox and with the big ends thumping their endless war dance underneath us, she flew up to London. John Greenfield never forgot the sight of Archie on his seat, relaxed and imperturbable, hands folded in his lap, his old cloth cap pulled well down and the mack with the coat tails flying in the wind. So we tore down Brentwood bank with steam on, crashing and lurching round the dog's hind leg at Gidea Park at just about line speed, on through Romford, Ilford, under the fly-over, past the Point and braking at last through Stratford. With a clear road, green lights as far as you could see, we ran through Bethnal Green and down the 1 in 70, still unchecked all the way into Liverpool Steet. Marvellous!

I never saw Archie again but he was a true Suffolker, a very good economical engineman who had the perfect temperament. He was a lovely man, never any trouble to anybody, spoke with a quiet, quavery voice and humorous smile. Always at peace with himself, he took life as it came, but, on the engine, he knew all the moves and was always a step ahead. And that was my last run on a 1500 in its natural environment and a fitting finale where even the old run-down 1566 ran her train to time and to spare. As for Johnny Greenfield, he never forgot Archie and his coat tails and he had a grandstand view standing behind the driver inches from the open space between cab and tender for the GER never got around to the idea of cab doors. As for me, how glad I am to be a member of the great brotherhood of railwaymen so that I can bring to mind hundreds indeed thousands of men in all grades who have made my life worth living.

The Railtour: 'Well, it really should not have happened!'

BY CHRIS BIRD

Remember, in 1963 the railway preservation movement was very much in its infancy and the M&GN Society had, hitherto, been just an idea and hope of a small band of keen railway enthusiasts to run a railway. The M&GN's 182-mile system was the first large-scale closure on the national network and certainly affected north Norfolk badly despite the increase in car ownership. This was the catalyst to save part of the M&GN system, although other lines were considered including the North Walsham to Mundesley branch. The volunteers were working without any precedent to follow. The Bluebell Railway had succeeded with its first season between 7 August and the end of October 1960, but was still very much a new thing. Our active members in those days probably did not exceed ten and there was nothing tangible apart from the name, as 'our' railway was yet to come. I suppose we could count ourselves as pioneers.

Despite lack of funds, as we had no meaningful earning ability plus the fact that disappearing steam had not then triggered the need to save some locomotives from the scrap men, we had made one important step forward. The two engines had been purchased from BR in late 1962 at the princely sum of £750 for the J15 and £1,500 for the B12 (was this amount a coincidence?). This seems a small sum now, but it was a giant step then. Actually the B12 fund was some £750 short and a loan was taken out with the locomotive as security because the Society was being pressurised to finalise the purchase. The monthly payments were made over two years with the result that the Society funds were painfully low on occasions. Shortly before purchase a steam test was arranged at Stratford Works, which was still in operation but in the process of being run down. We were very lucky as the Works foreman was a keen steam man and had unofficially ensured that both engines were in full working order before the test. In addition, Bill Harvey at Norwich shed had given the B12 a lot of care whilst there before eventually surrendering 'his' engine under pressure from BR's Eastern Region headquarters. Needless to say both locomotives passed the tests with flying colours, although one point did get missed which did not come to light until the day of the tour.

61572 in Devon's Road shed yard in September 1963. Only a few weeks later the loco would be pressed into service for the first time in two years.
DAVID BUTCHER

The impressive frontage of
Broad Street station, 1961.
BEN BROOKSBANK

The B12 and J15 then needed a home. As one person commented, 'we can't have them wrapped up and taken home'. BR, bless them, agreed to them being stored at Devons Road depot in East London. This was the first all-diesel depot on BR, but was being run down whilst we were there and closed in 1964. The allocation of locomotives (mainly Class 21s) was transferred to Willesden. The depot was finally demolished in 1983 and the area is now an industrial estate.

I acted as rider when they were towed from Stratford. I remember clearly on this journey crossing over a new skew bridge over the A12 at Victoria Park and passing through Old Ford and Bow stations. I recollect that the station signs were still hanging from the platform gas lamps, which is amazing as they had closed to passengers in 1945. I wonder what happened to them? This is an impossible journey now, as the section from Victoria Park Junction southward to the point where it passed under the Great Eastern main line is no more, closing completely in 1967. South of this and past where Devons Road depot was sited is now part of the Docklands light railway. Electricity was still live in the depot after closure and, following repairs to one of the main doors, half was made pretty secure. It did seem very odd to have a ten- road shed to ourselves complete with electric lights at nil cost to the Society.

Being the proud owners of 65462 and 61572 it seemed right to show them off to a wider audience. Working parties were organised to progress maintenance on both engines. The Society decided it would be a good idea if the B12 could be used to haul a railtour and it was left to me to see what could be done (I was working in the Traffic Manager's Office – Hamilton House – Liverpool Street at the time). First, I decided that the tour should start from as near to the B12's current home as possible. As it had a route availability of 4, that is it could go many places on the rail network though not all, some interesting secondary routes were a possibility (I have to admit to being a branch line fan). It seemed sensible to avoid any tender first running if possible and to plan a route that was practical for a day trip. So out came my atlas and the following seemed a good balance. Start from Broad Street (This was London Midland Region territory as was Devons Road), then Dalston Junction, Finsbury Park, East Coast main line, Hitchin, Bedford Midland Road, Northampton Castle (run round), Blisworth (run round), Towcester, Stratford-upon-Avon, Hatton, Leamington Spa, Birdingbury (what a lovely name), Rugby, West Coast main line, Primrose Hill, and back to Broad Street. How about a name for the tour? I was talking one weekend at home in Cambridge about the tour with my mother – she thought I was distinctly unhinged with my interest in dirty steam engines, however both of my parents came on the trip – and she came up with the idea of 'Wandering 1500'. This seemed appropriate in view of the route and so it was chosen.

I then contacted the Traffic Manager's office at Euston and had a long chat with the Special Traffic section as the proposed start point was on their 'patch'. They were very keen and set the wheels in motion and the date was duly set, timings and costs worked out and tickets printed. The B12 was to be hauled across to Willesden a few days beforehand, serviced, checked and the fire lit. I must have been a very lucky soul as no one queried the use of the locomotive and only a couple of points threatened the arrangements. First, the timing office phoned me and said they were worried that the cylinders might foul the platform at Blisworth when running round. A quick re-assurance was given that the engine had inside cylinders and was not a problem. I thought it wise not to ask what engine drawing they were looking at. And they went away quite happy. The other 'mini panic' was a few days before the tour when I had a phone call from the shed foreman at Willesden. 'Your loco can't go out unless I get the gauge glass protectors pronto' – I do not think he was very happy having a 'foreign' engine on shed. My boss at the time said, 'go and sort them out'. A hasty trip to Ilford (where I was lodging) to collect them (removed for safe keeping) and a dash to Willesden depot put that right. This was followed by, 'whilst

> **"** They were worried that the cylinders might foul the platform at Blisworth ... re-assurance was given that the engine had inside cylinders and was not a problem. **"**

you are here, son, (I was only 22 at the time) what do you know about the Westinghouse air pump, its stuck?' Luckily I had learned a bit: 'get a dish of paraffin and a hammer'. Hitting the side a few times moved the piston and with the dish under the air inlet it drew the paraffin into the cylinder, then a top up with engine oil and it was back in business. Huge sigh of relief – the less people that knew what was going on the better.

The day of the tour dawned dry and quite mild and I arrived at Broad Street just before 61572 backed on to our train – eight LMS bogies which had been brought in by a Peak diesel locomotive. The crew on this were very good and had shut it down so there was not any diesel noise. Bang on time we were off with a good compliment of passengers, not full but enough to make a profit in the low hundreds of pounds. We were soon at Finsbury Park where a short stop was made to take on water from a very leaky crane. Somewhere after this stop it was discovered that there was a leak in the steam heating pipe that runs through the tender (the item that was missed at the steam test) but luckily it was a mild day. Off down the fast line taking it fairly steady to allow the motion to bed in – it was now on a real run, a first for some years. Remember the B12 was withdrawn on 20 September 1961 and there was not an opportunity for a test run beforehand. There was a brief stop at Hitchin and then on to the Bedford branch. From Bedford there was a short run north on the Midland main line to Oakley Junction where we branched left towards Northampton, passing through Bridge Street on our way to Castle station where the engine was uncoupled. It was originally intended to avoid Northampton by branching left at Ravenstone Wood Junction and going through Stoke Bruerne (of canal fame) to Towcester. This was thwarted as the branch was being used to store some 100 wagons, which would have been difficult to move elsewhere. A quick visit to the engine shed was needed to top up coal and clean the fire with 'yours truly' on the footplate. It was here that disaster nearly struck. We pulled forward in the depot and Dave Butcher shouted and we ground to a very abrupt halt. The front bogie had split a set of points. We set back and all was well. Thank goodness for air brakes. There were a number of very young train spotters about who wanted to cab the locomotive, which was arranged. As we left the depot to

The hastily produced tour schedule.
DAVID BUTCHER

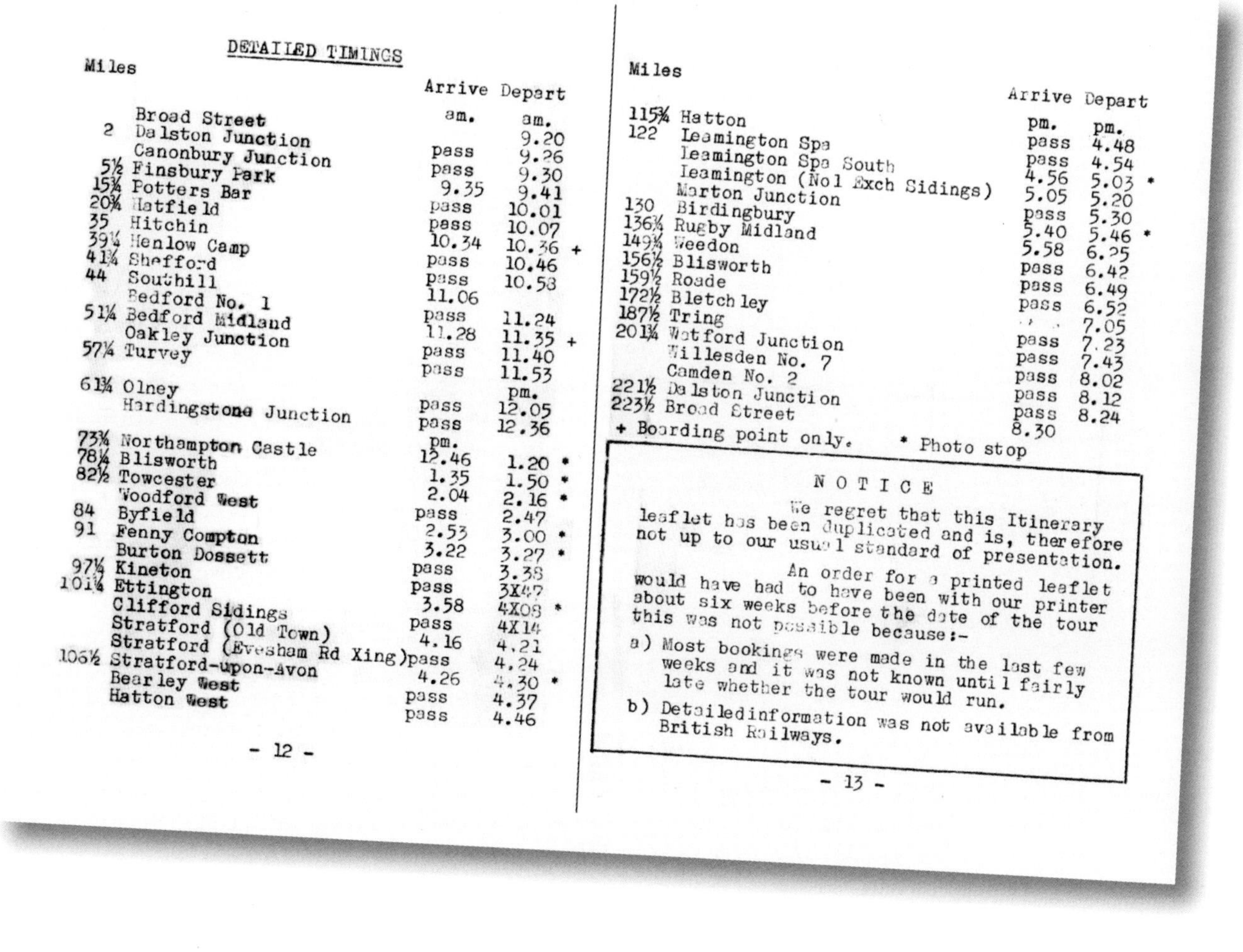

DETAILED TIMINGS

Miles		Arrive	Depart	
	Broad Street	am.	am.	
2	Dalston Junction		9.20	
	Canonbury Junction	pass	9.26	
5½	Finsbury Park	pass	9.30	
15¾	Potters Bar	9.35	9.41	
20¾	Hatfield	pass	10.01	
35	Hitchin	pass	10.07	
39¼	Henlow Camp	10.34	10.36	+
41¾	Shefford	pass	10.46	
44	Southill	pass	10.58	
	Bedford No. 1	11.06		
51¼	Bedford Midland	pass	11.24	
	Oakley Junction	11.28	11.35	+
57¼	Turvey	pass	11.40	
		pass	11.53	
61¾	Olney		pm.	
	Hardingstone Junction	pass	12.05	
		pass	12.36	
73¾	Northampton Castle	pm.		
78¼	Blisworth	12.46	1.20	*
82½	Towcester	1.35	1.50	*
	Woodford West	2.04	2.16	*
84	Byfield	pass	2.47	
91	Fenny Compton	2.53	3.00	*
	Burton Dossett	3.22	3.27	*
97¼	Kineton	pass	3.38	
101¼	Ettington	pass	3X47	
	Clifford Sidings	3.58	4X08	*
	Stratford (Old Town)	pass	4X14	
	Stratford (Evesham Rd Xing)	4.16	4.21	
106½	Stratford-upon-Avon	pass	4.24	
	Bearley West	4.26	4.30	*
	Hatton West	pass	4.37	
		pass	4.46	

- 12 -

Miles		Arrive	Depart	
115¾	Hatton	pm.	pm.	
122	Leamington Spa	pass	4.48	
	Leamington Spa South	pass	4.54	
	Leamington (No1 Exch Sidings)	4.56	5.03	*
	Marton Junction	5.05	5.20	
130	Birdingbury	pass	5.30	
136¾	Rugby Midland	5.40	5.46	*
149¾	Weedon	5.58	6.25	
156½	Blisworth	pass	6.42	
159½	Roade	pass	6.49	
172½	Bletchley	pass	6.52	
187½	Tring	[illegible]	7.05	
201¾	Watford Junction	pass	7.23	
	Willesden No. 7	pass	7.43	
	Camden No. 2	pass	8.02	
221½	Dalston Junction	pass	8.12	
223½	Broad Street	pass	8.24	
		8.30		

+ Boarding point only. * Photo stop

NOTICE

We regret that this Itinerary leaflet has been duplicated and is, therefore not up to our usual standard of presentation.

An order for a printed leaflet would have had to have been with our printer about six weeks before the date of the tour this was not possible because:-

a) Most bookings were made in the last few weeks and it was not known until fairly late whether the tour would run.

b) Detailedinformation was not available from British Railways.

- 13 -

head back to Castle station we could see them huddled together over their ABC books wondering why they could not find 61572 – smiles all round.

Off we went tender first to Blisworth and a further run round to gain the Stratford-upon-Avon and Midland Junction Railway. Our engine had settled down and we were away up the bank on a left hand curve with some very reassuring sounds from the chimney. Brief stops at Towcester and Byfield followed and over the Great Western main line to arrive at Fenny Compton. Unfortunately a suitable guard had not been rostered for the next section so we had about an hour's wait. Then we were on to Stratford Old Town where it was necessary to set back before proceeding into Stratford itself. No further problems were encountered until Leamington Spa where it was necessary to shunt the train from General to Milverton to gain access to the London and North Western route to Rugby. As we were late the photo stop at Birdingbury was omitted and we duly arrived in the Up platform at Rugby. It was decided that the fire needed a good clean, at least partly due to the long wait at Fenny Compton, which would lengthen 61572's time on shed. I went through the train (for the second time) to explain the delay. As we were going to be a further 45 minutes late, at least, an extra stop was arranged at Watford Junction to set down passengers. After the engine was recoupled we were given a bit of a challenge – do we wait for the express to pass in about 20 minutes or go first? 'Go first' was the decision. Off we went from Rugby, main line all the way south to Watford Junction. A splendid run followed with speeds of over 70 mph keeping us well ahead of the express. The start away from Watford Junction was truly memorable with the very sharp exhaust echoing off adjacent buildings. And so we arrived back at Broad Street at 10.45pm, about two hours late. The station was kept open specially and the supervisor asked the engine crew where they had been (or words to that effect). The locomotive proved itself in a wonderful way and the sounds of some of the starts have remained with me to this day. I had to depart rather quickly after the tour finished in order to catch the last train from King's Cross to Cambridge, a 3 × 2 car Cravens DMU – what a come down!

61572 was returned to Devons Road and when I visited the following week was still quite warm.

I have been asked why the coupling rods were painted red as appeared in photographs of the trip. It was very much a GER tradition to do this, but I really do not remember when or who did so before the tour.

There was also the 'story' going round that BR did not know the locomotive was not theirs until the tour was underway. I can confirm this is partly true. BR Eastern Region of course sold the engines to the Society and it was a different department that organised the trip. I spoke to them in fair detail about the B12, but nothing was put in writing and, luckily for the tour, the whole conversation was ignored. As the work done at Stratford was unofficial and the B12 was not shown as re-instated it was still a scrap locomotive on BR's records.

Makes me cringe what we got away with and not something I have been keen to repeat. Luckily, we knew 61572 was okay, otherwise our enthusiasm at the time would have been checked by the niceties of ensuring the engine was 'fit for purpose'. I had been re-assured that the boiler certificate was current, but had not managed to obtain a copy – was there actually a certificate or was this another 'story'? If Health and Safety had been around then they would have had a field day!

The follow up was to be a trip over the Somerset & Dorset with the B12. Word had got round that the locomotive had been out and about and was to haul the second special. My mailbag was overwhelming! However, senior people within BR had got to know about the Wandering 1500s exploits and were, quite rightly, asking all sorts of questions. We were refused permission – hardly surprisingly bearing the above in mind – to use our engine on the follow up tour but were offered two 'Castles' as a replacement. It was

> **"After the engine was recoupled we were given a bit of a challenge – do we wait for the express to pass in about 20 minutes or go first?"**

The big day, the tour is seen approaching Towcester.
TOMMY TOMALIN

Still warm! On shed at Willesden the day after the tour and still carrying the 1X69 train working board.
GEOFF RIXON

decided to cancel as all booking requests were expecting 61572 and not a substitute. With the benefit of hindsight I think this was a mistake. We should have explained, run the trip and ploughed any profit into the Society coffers.

Undoubtedly the tour was a Society high point and did much to keep spirits and determination alive. It is a tribute to the perseverance of all involved that the section of M&GN between Sheringham and Weybourne was opened and followed later by the extension to Holt. The B12 had to wait to be steamed again until the re-dedication at Sheringham on 3 March 1995 following a major overhaul in Germany, nearly 32 years after the 'Wandering 1500' tour.

Finally, it is interesting to note that a good portion of the route taken has now gone. The front part of Broad Street station was demolished in summer 1985 and the site now forms part of the Broadgate development. The section to Dalston Junction finally closed completely on 30 June 1986, but has recently reopened as part of the East London railway extension. Other sections to disappear were: Oakley Junction to Northampton Bridge Street; the short section to Castle is still there, but heavily over grown; Castle station to Blisworth; the SMJ to Stratford – except for a section from Fenny Compton to Kineton to serve the MOD depot; and Leamington Spa to Rugby – except for a very short section at the Rugby end.

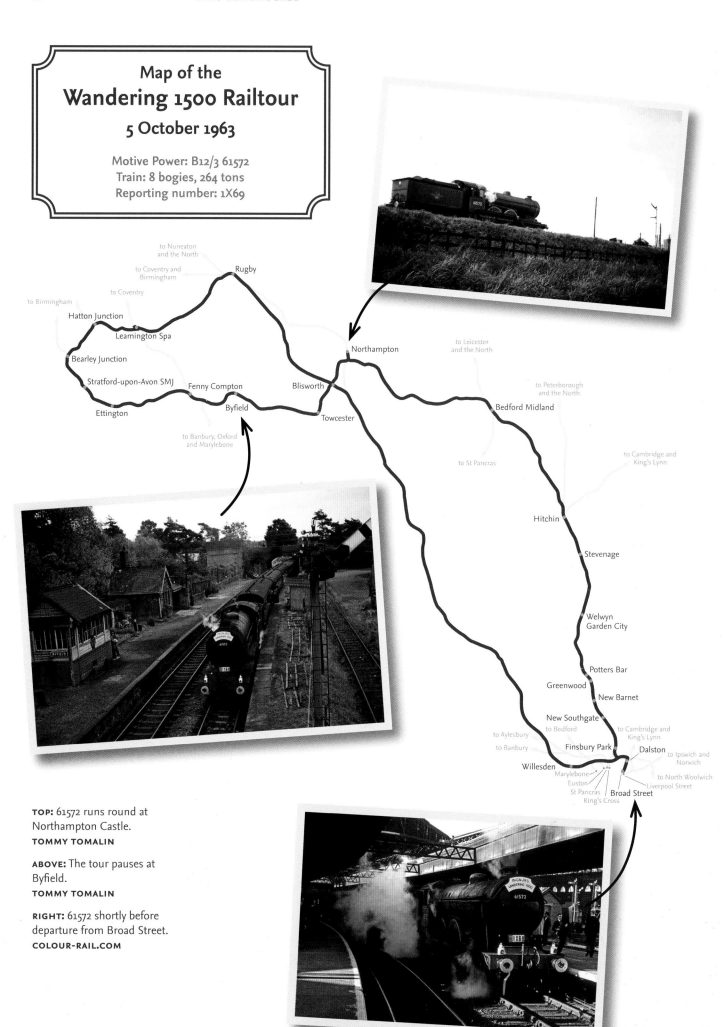

Map of the
Wandering 1500 Railtour
5 October 1963

Motive Power: B12/3 61572
Train: 8 bogies, 264 tons
Reporting number: 1X69

to Nuneaton and the North

Rugby

to Coventry and Birmingham

to Coventry

to Birmingham

Hatton Junction

Leamington Spa

Northampton

to Leicester and the North

Bearley Junction

Stratford-upon-Avon SMJ

Fenny Compton

Blisworth

to Peterborough and the North

Bedford Midland

Ettington

Byfield

Towcester

to Cambridge and King's Lynn

to Banbury, Oxford and Marylebone

to St Pancras

Hitchin

Stevenage

Welwyn Garden City

Potters Bar

Greenwood

New Barnet

New Southgate

to Aylesbury

to Bedford

to Cambridge and King's Lynn

Dalston

to Banbury

Finsbury Park

to Ipswich and Norwich

Willesden

Marylebone

to North Woolwich

Euston

Liverpool Street

St Pancras

Broad Street

King's Cross

TOP: 61572 runs round at Northampton Castle.
TOMMY TOMALIN

ABOVE: The tour pauses at Byfield.
TOMMY TOMALIN

RIGHT: 61572 shortly before departure from Broad Street.
COLOUR-RAIL.COM

The Wandering 1500 Railtour: 5 October 1963

BY DAVID BUTCHER

I was in my office attending to routine paperwork, just after returning from lunch on a Friday afternoon. The phone rang, in itself nothing unusual, until an unfamiliar voice quietly asked 'Is that you, Butcher?' The voice was clearly one of importance and authority, and one to be given due respect. This was quickly confirmed. 'Yes, sir.'

'I understand you formerly worked on the B12 1500s, is that correct?' 'Yes, sir.'

'We have a slight problem, and I'm told you might help us.' 'Yes, sir.'

'We have 1572, which has not worked for a couple of years, being brought out of storage to work a railtour tomorrow. Can you get to Willesden shed tomorrow morning, early?' 'Yes, sir.'

'Our inspector will be on the engine. I will tell him to look out for you.' 'Yes, sir.'

'Your presence is strictly unofficial. Do not report to the shed authorities, but make your way direct to the engine. It would be wiser not to say who you really are. Do you still have your engine overalls?' 'Yes, sir.'

'Good, then I suggest you wear them'. 'Yes, sir.'

This is a decently accurate retelling of one of the most unusual telephone calls I was to receive during my years as a manager. I had previously enquired if it might be possible to have a pass to ride on the engine. I did not really expect to be granted one, but upon the premise of nothing ventured, nothing gained, had decided to ask just in case.

I never did discover if my request was overtaken by events, or if it triggered this unusual call. It did not really matter anyway. I was now going with the blessing of higher authority. My trip was to be in a semi-official, unofficial capacity, if this makes any sense.

61572 makes a spirited departure from Broad Street.
MIKE MORANT

Shortly after leaving Broad Street, '72 gets into its stride as it passes through Dalston Junction station with steam to spare.

COLOUR-RAIL.COM

The morning of Saturday, 5 October 1963, dawned bright and clear. Remarkably it was to remain so for most of what became a very enjoyable and memorable day. Mother nature was to remind us who was boss, providing a few rain showers to add a touch of down-to-earth reality.

1572 stood out in the open simmering nicely in the early morning sunshine, a fair distance away from the Willesden shed building, looking clean and ready for work. I had not seen it since the day, when walking north of Copper Mill junction, it passed *en route* to Liverpool Street on a special working. I believe it was 1572's final appearance in London in normal service. How, or why, it came to be on this duty, I have not the slightest idea. It was a fair guess, though, that the hand of the late Bill Harvey, then shedmaster at Norwich, was involved in it somewhere!

Making my way with an air of complete innocence and looking as if this was a normal everyday thing to do, I approached the engine. A clearly anxious inspector climbed down off the engine to make his way towards me. 'Are you who I think you are?' was his non-committal opening greeting, just in case I was not. 'Yes, I think I am.'

'Thank goodness for that. I was rung at home last night to be told someone familiar with the engine would be riding today, to help out. Who are you by the way?'

In this manner, I made the acquaintance of Inspector Bill Lockwood from Stratford. I quickly got the impression he could not be far from retirement. He certainly had no desire to be firing the engine but would had 'push come to shove' in *dire extremis*. We were to get on very well together as the day progressed.

"A clearly anxious inspector climbed down off the engine ... 'Are you who I think you are?' was his non-committal opening greeting, just in case I was not. 'Yes, I think I am.'"

These important preliminaries over, and with his tacit agreement to withhold my true identity; we climbed on the engine. Suitable introductions to the Willesden men, who were to work as far as Northampton, were made. I was explained away as being involved with the engine, riding out on my day off. All of which was entirely true. In more modern times, such a subterfuge has become known as 'being economical with the truth'.

The booked fireman readily agreed for me to do the firing because, as he said 'I know nuffin about her, bruv'. (Union members called each other 'brother'). We quickly started to get the old lady into a fit state for the day ahead. The driver had no knowledge of the air brake, nor had Willesden the required thicker oil for the Westinghouse donkey pump, so ordinary cylinder oil had to suffice. We had the smokebox open, we checked the ashpan and in particular the drop grate to ensure it was fully shut, also that the air reservoirs were empty of water. I built up a decent fire whilst the fireman filled the tender with water and trimmed the coal. The front was wiped over (that is, the back of the boiler inside the cab) and the copper pipework rubbed up to remove the excess of two years dirt and grime. It was scheduled to be our home for the next 14 hours, and I never could tolerate a dirty cab.

We had nearly 260 miles ahead of us, Willesden to Willesden, *via* middle England. Not dissimilar to working a train from King's Cross to Newcastle, 268 miles, which is something a '1500' has never done! Indeed, it crosses my mind to wonder if, just possibly, this is the longest distance ever rostered to be worked by one in a single working day. I would imagine it is with one train on a continuous journey if not for a full day's work. What a way to celebrate the very last run by one in BR ownership, if this is the case. Our first real chance to replenish the coal was to be at Rugby, some 11 hours hence. We prepared for a long day.

In no time at all, at least that is what it seemed, we were ringing out at the shed outlet signal at 8.20am to run light engine, tender first, to Broad Street. Initially, '72 creaked and groaned until the mechanical lubricator began getting oil into the parts we could not reach during the preparation. Bill had trickled a little cylinder oil down the blastpipe when we checked the smokebox to give her a start. By the time we reached Broad Street she was beginning to sound a little better. As we slowly backed on to the train, the platform was swarming with our passengers. Cameras were clicking away thirteen to the dozen. During our run up from Willesden I had continued to steadily build up the fire at the front end of the box, with quizzical looks from our fireman.

'You haven't built up the back corners,' he queried.

'No, that's right,' I replied.

'Why is that?'

'Because this old lady has an appetite up the front and prefers a thinner fire at the back.'

He found this difficult to comprehend. This was one of Eastern Region's worries, that the Midland crew would 'lump her' and then be in trouble for steam. Bill maintained a diplomatic silence, and the driver simply smiled. 'Little and often' firing techniques to a thinnish fire bed rarely figured in the methodology of Midland men, well used to 'filling them up and flogging them hard' as the saying went.

Their engines were mainly fitted with deeper fireboxes that could carry a good depth of fire bed. 1572, in common with many other GE designs, has a shallow firebox that has to

Greenwood, some two and a half miles before Potters Bar.
T A MURPHY/
COLOUR-RAIL.COM BRE928

be fired with a fair degree of skill for best results. This ensured that the full heat value was abstracted from each knob of coal, with minimum effort, and hence fairly economical coal usage relative to the work being done. The old GER was frugal with its coal bills!

Our driver had meanwhile been having a useful chat with Bill about the best way to handle her. 'How much regulator and what degree of cut off on the reverser does she like?' was typical of the discussion taking place on the opposite side of the engine while our fireman and I were similarly getting acquainted on our side.

Up came the guard. 'What's this we've got here, driver?' The donkey pump was doing its thing in the background as he spoke. 'Sounds like a road traction engine to me, mate – have you brought the plough?' he enquired!

The driver professed he was not sure what he had, but said 'We'll be alright, pal – yer just sit at the rear with yer flags and whistle and make sure the handbrake is fully off.' Typical railway humour exchanged with the banter of each participant defending his corner! Our eight-coach formation was advised as 264 tons tare, say 290 tons total weight with our full complement of passengers.

At 9.20am sharp, with platform staff whistling up the last photographers as they scrambled aboard, we popped the whistle and got under way. It was a voyage of discovery. None of us knew what state she was really in, nor what the next few miles would tell us while we got the measure of 1572. She was certainly very stiff and reluctant to run freely – hardly surprising after being out of use for so long. We were signalled over the No. 1 Lines as we left Broad Street behind us.

It was nice to hear the bark of a '1500' sounding over Liverpool Street when it was assumed it could never happen again. By the time we passed Skinner Street box, with its grandstand view over the entire area of the Great Eastern terminus below and the North London terminus above, 1572 was beginning to get into its stride. Our driver was starting to smile as he began to feel the strength of her. Later in the trip he was to comment again about this. We ran steadily along the lengthy viaduct at Haggerston and carried gently on until the steep grade down off it before Dalston Junction, to regain *terra firma* once more. Whistling up for the junction station as we carefully approached, then running through alongside the sharply curved platform, caused several surprised faces to look at us. Through Dalston Western Junction we went, past the site of Mildmay Park station and then through Canonbury station, also with interested onlookers. Before long we were slowing for the Canonbury Junction turn off and into the long Canonbury Tunnel to emerge back into the sunshine up through Highbury Vale and alongside the then Northern Line Moorgate branch of London Underground. A steady climb, under the Great Northern main line,

Having run up the East Coast main line, 61572 rolls into Hitchin station. After taking on water, the tour took the Midland line to Bedford.
THE LATE M THOMPSON/ COLOUR-RAIL.COM

61572 at speed near Bedford.
A E DURRANT/MIKE MORANT
COLLECTION

past Clarence Yard and into Finsbury Park then followed for our first water stop. We were also booked to take on our first pilotman.

Up stepped a King's Cross man, well known to me. Before he recovered from his surprise, it was possible to catch his eye and signal not to say anything! During the trip a discreet exchange explained matters and we exchanged wry smiles. I knew I could rely on his discretion. I had fired for him in my past life. We had several trips together, from good to not so good. Today was going to be one of the latter sort to start with.

Departing from Finsbury Park we were turned out main line. We were about to find out what our venerable old lady was capable of doing. Initially 1572 was going well. Up the rise to Harringay West and then down through the long sweeping curves past Hornsey and on to Wood Green I was in control. She seemed to be steaming alright, yet instinct said all was not as it should be. Sensing all might not be quite right I had got a good glassfull of water in her by Wood Green. These suspicions were soon confirmed. I knew the road, l knew our pilotman's driving style, I knew the engine. None of it helped.

Before long the feeling of being in control was slipping away, without understanding why. By the time we were passing New Southgate, well into the climb to Potters Bar, the needle was beginning to ease ever so slowly, but ever so surely, back from the red line. It became a process of attrition to balance the need for the boiler injectors against falling steam pressure. She was definitely sounding laboured, although pulling well. In normal service she would have been on the red line. The fire was right, it was bright and in good fettle. There was no need to interfere with it. We had a good, lightish grey haze from the chimney. A glance to Bill Lockwood confirmed that he was not unduly concerned. We both knew what 1572 was capable of in adverse circumstances when one is forced to mortgage the boiler water level a little to eke out the steam supply. By New Barnet we were down to 150 lbs/sq in pressure with two thirds of a glass of water. Not satisfactory but it could have been worse. A quick look at the driver, who was also entirely unfamiliar with the '1500s', was rewarded with a knowing wink. We approached the summit at Potters Bar with pressure down to 135 lbs/sq in and the water by now well down in the glass. We had run at a fairly steady 40 to 45mph throughout the eight miles of the 1 in 200 rising gradient. Turning the summit, despite our lack of pressure and water, confirmed that barring an unforeseen situation we could, hopefully, keep the flag flying for the rest of the day. A heartening reassurance.

Our Willesden crew had tactfully remained silent throughout the long climb until now. As we went through Potters Bar station with its unusual and ugly sagging concrete roof canopies, I turned on both injectors as the driver eased the regulator almost shut. The Willesden driver then offered his comment to say how surprised he was with the

After five miles of tender first running from Northampton, the tour is seen at Blisworth before heading (smokebox first) along the SMJ.
TOMMY TOMALIN

ability of 1572 to keep going so strongly in such an adverse situation. He may not have been over impressed with my effort, but he certainly was with that of the engine. We had cheated just a wee bit by turning off the donkey pump to save steam on the climb. Fortunately, we had no steam heating on otherwise that would have gone too! We discovered she held the air pressure better than expected – a minor bonus. With the water now well down in the lower half of the glass and with the first port of the regulator only half open, we soon began to gather speed while still holding the pressure steady at 135lbs/sq in, down towards Brookmans Park with the worst behind us. Back to a more healthy two thirds of a glass of water as we were approaching Marshmoor box, one injector was turned off to help boiler pressure recover. By Hatfield we had a far more respectable 160 lbs/sq in on the clock. It did not go below this for the rest of the trip to Hitchin. For eight miles, from Hadley Wood until after Hatfield, I had not touched the shovel – it was not necessary to do so. I hoped my credentials had risen slightly in the eyes of the Willesden men when they saw the situation steadily improve without any further firing. Clearly there could not have been too much wrong with the fire for this to be possible. When one is under scrutiny from fellow professionals it is not always easy to maintain the required outward show of confidence. Pride is a vital ingredient among the engineman's repertoire of skills.

By Welwyn Garden City we were beginning to run much more freely as the oil was getting around her. Then came a caution before sighting Woolmer Green's splitting distants, located between the two Welwyn tunnels, with the left hand one pulled off to turn us into the slow road. We were through Knebworth and well on to Langley when a Down express came by on the main line. We earned a toot on the whistle and a friendly wave from the crew as they overtook us. We had not delayed them. We ran on through Stevenage and had a good run on down to Hitchin South box, to be held there for a couple of minutes while another train cleared the station platform ahead of us. The improved smoothness of our running was suggesting the old lady had finally re-awoken from her

Pulling hard as 61572 climbs out of Blisworth.
TOMMY TOMALIN

rudely interrupted slumbers of the last couple of years or so since official withdrawal from traffic. She seemed to have caught the mood of the occasion and was to behave well for the rest of the day, apart from one more little sulk after departing from Blisworth.

At Hitchin we said cheerio to our King's Cross driver to welcome aboard a Bedford driver as our new pilotman. He had travelled out *via* Sandy and Cambridge to reach Hitchin! (The direct line was closed to passenger trains.) After topping up the tender tank, and letting her pose for the bevy of photographers that surrounded her on the platform, it was time once more to get under way. We were running only a little behind schedule, which for a railtour is usually an achievement. Covering the gently undulating grades through Henlow Camp and beyond to Cardington and Bedford, we ran under light steam to reclaim some of the lost minutes on the scheduled timings for this section. The large airship sheds built on the RAF camp at Cardington brought back strong personal memories recalling that I had initially reported there ten years previously to commence my National Service. To step inside those vast structures was quite an awe-inspiring experience. Such thoughts quickly dissipated as we approached Bedford Midland station over the unusual flat rail crossing. This in turn recalled yet further memories of the nearby station of Bedford St Johns. I had last been over this crossing with a Bletchley to Cambridge working, nearly eleven years previously – it now seemed odd to be doing it on the opposite route. What a day for memories it was turning out to be!

Joining the main line out of St Pancras, we stopped at Midland station to pick up the last of our passengers. After taking on water we had a short gallop over the one and a half miles to Oakley Junction before branching off left to set our smokebox pointing for Turvey and Northampton.

We soon encountered a nasty little climb, surmounted in decent style, although the old lady again became shy for steam when the second regulator valve was used. Drawing into Northampton Castle station we were booked onto the shed to take water and have a general check around. All bearings were perfectly cool. A quick oiling up and we were ready to run round the train prior to working tender first for the five miles to Blisworth. We also said farewell to our Bedford driver and the Willesden crew – the fireman kindly expressing his thanks for my efforts on his behalf.

After giving the coal a good soaking with the slacker pipe (or 'pep pipe' as GE men called it) we set off with a fresh Northampton crew in charge. The new fireman said he was happy for me to continue and explained there was a steep bank to climb after leaving Blisworth. The fire bed was accordingly built up in readiness. As we ran tender first it rained – very inconsiderate! By Blisworth this had cleared. We ran into the station to run round to face the proper direction of travel, with engine leading, before shunting over onto the ex-SMJ (Stratford-upon-Avon and Midland Junction Railway) exchange sidings

> to gain the SMJ branch. Again the fireman emphasised the steep bank ahead of us. So yet again I gave the fire a final check round to ensure all was according to plan. We departed with a good glassful of water and the needle on the red line. And we were running nearly to schedule – it was too good to be true!

" She was pulling strongly. So strongly, in fact, that our new driver refused to believe the power classification code '4P' "

Yet again, as soon as the driver got her into her stride and opened up the second valve on the regulator as we attacked the foot of the bank, the steam pressure began to go the wrong way. It was odd because there was no apparent reason. The exhaust beats were strong and even, there was no unusual blow that we could detect and she was pulling strongly. So strongly, in fact, that our new driver refused to believe the power classification code '4P' painted on the cab side claiming she was far stronger than a '4' rating! He became even more amused when the pressure dropped back to 140lbs/sq in with little difference to 1572's ability to pound on up the bank. She was taking it in fine style at 20 to 25mph. She sounded beautiful and to the outside observer, in fine form. Apart from checking the fire to confirm everything was in order, it was not necessary to fire. The pressure continued to fall back. Eventually the water level required a top up to keep a good third of a glass in place, which did the pressure no good at all. By now I was asking the fireman 'How much further up the bank?' The old lady was still doing her bit and barking away nicely. 'About a quarter mile' came the reply. I let her run with the injector still on. I saw him looking at the pressure gauge and thought 'any second now and the vacuum will start to go on'. We were down to 110 lbs/sq in as we breasted the summit, with the water level well down, but we were safe as we surmounted the top. The regulator was eased as she began to recover.

Stopping at Towcester shortly afterwards quickly restored both water level and pressure. It was most odd – we were quickly okay once again. As at Potters Bar, immediately the regulator was eased back to first valve the pressure had recovered. The fire was in good shape and needed no attention. Since leaving Broad Street I had not touched a fire-iron and had no intention of doing so. I had always eschewed the use of these ungainly weapons out on the road, preferring to fire myself out of trouble if at all possible. Occasionally you had to concede and use them, but it could cause a fire to clinker up if you were not careful

The Wandering 1500 passes through the closed Blakesley station.
M SMITH/COLOUR-RAIL.COM

With the weather taking a turn for the worse, the tour passes through Ettington.
COLOUR-RAIL.COM

and sparing in their use. The Northampton fireman wanted to put the pricker through the firebed; I advised against it, and fortunately he agreed. Remember, I was an extra member on the footplate although the presence of our inspector regularised the situation.

At Towcester we posed for a scheduled photo stop in fine weather. Our frequent whistling aroused the curiosity of the locals who had not seen a passenger train for a very long time! We resumed our journey on through Woodford West and over the Great Central main line as the weather began to deteriorate. We pulled into Fenny Compton station, by now back on schedule, in steady rain. The Gods, until then, had smiled down upon us – now Nemesis struck! There was no pilotman waiting on the platform for our guard who did not sign for the road beyond Fenny (as it was known in railway parlance). This had been arranged by telegram the previous day to Birmingham. They had slipped up and overlooked it. And there we waited, and waited, and waited . . . for well over an hour. The fire was now showing signs of the mileage that had passed since leaving Willesden. We did consider cleaning it out a bit, but this might have done more harm than good, so we kept the fire doors shut to prevent cold air reaching the tubeplate more than necessary. Eventually our pilot guard arrived and we were again on our way. The DMU that had brought him promptly became a failure in the station, but fortunately this did not affect us. We moved off before Control got any notions about using our engine to assist – we had yet to reach the halfway mark of the tour! It was now late afternoon. The countryside through which we were passing was quite delightful. It was like being on an old-fashioned charabanc trip with the air swirling around you through the open sides as we gently ambled along despite the rain – in our case to the music of rail joints over the almost disused single line. It was due for early closure and we were to be the last passenger working over it, so we were told. I cannot confirm this.

In due course we pulled into Stratford-upon-Avon SMJ station, long since closed to passengers on 7 April 1952. I recall visiting the adjoining engine shed on Sunday 6 April, following the actual cessation of passenger traffic the previous day. Midland Railway 3F 43822 was on shed with the last rites still chalked around and on the smokebox door. I particularly recalled the steeply angled wooden canopy awning over one of the platforms and was hoping this unusual feature might still be extant. Alas, it had gone, the station was semi-derelict and the platforms barely usable. We took water from the old-fashioned fixed column that survived between the running lines in the station amidst still more photos as the rain had now cleared.

Our delay at Fenny had not yet snowballed into further delays but it was soon to do so, despite some energetic running beyond Fenny. We regained 15 minutes to Stratford only to see a Birmingham express precede us, so we promptly lost them again. We were booked *via* the Bearley junctions, Hatton and Warwick to Leamington Spa station. The delays began to build up and we eventually arrived at Leamington now well down on schedule. Here a further shunt was necessary to reach the next section *via* the former LNWR exchange sidings. This was yet another backwater of a single line to Rugby, used for part of its length to serve the Long Itchington cement works, near Rugby. These trains joined our route at Marton Junction where we continued on *via* Dunchurch to reach Rugby. This branch was yet another to have lost its passenger services. Dr Beeching's era was not the only one to cut back the post-war railway system.

As we commenced our journey over the branch I was kindly offered the chance to have hold of the engine to Rugby. The Northampton lad did the firing over this sedate stretch of interesting line. Yet again, more memories! I had last travelled over it in 1949 behind a London and North Western Railway Webb 2-4-2 tank on the push-and-pull motor unit that had worked this service for many years. They were just about to surrender to the new Ivatt 1200 series 2MT 2-6-2 tanks. Some of these had been motor fitted to work with, and later replace, the Webb tanks during the summer of 1949. I had journeyed behind a Webb tank just in time before they finally disappeared from the line.

Upon arrival at Rugby we were booked to go on shed to give the engine a much needed service. She required oiling up, fire cleaning, ashpan and smokebox emptying, re-coaling and watering. We had a good run ahead of us to Willesden Junction. It was essential to be in proper shape. Never has an engine been serviced so quickly! A half hour had been allowed, which was totally impossible to achieve, but we had a good go at doing all the requirements within the hour. Whilst our passengers sought replenishment in the station buffet – it was now getting dark – we sweated (and be it whispered, cursed a little too) to replenish our old lady's state of health. We shovelled some hefty chunks of clinker out by hand, to avoid any risk of the drop grate jamming as we used it, before preparing the fire. By the time we came off shed to back onto our train the station lights were on. Our Northampton crew had headed for home and now we had a set of Rugby top link main line men in charge. They were as keen as mustard to 'try out this strange machine with the windy pump dangling on the side footplating' as our new fireman summarised his impression of our venerable engine. By now Bill Lockwood and I had fallen under her spell. She had performed well except when pushed hard with the second regulator valve open. Our Rugby man who had so cheekily insulted our truly wandering engine was eager to have a go. I had done all the firing from Willesden, now some 13 hours behind us, as far as Leamington. I suggested he fired her to my instruction regarding firebed depth. I explained the 'lump her and sit back for a breather' style would not work. Bill was having a quiet word with the driver as to driving style. They agreed to use first valve only as far as possible, with a slightly increased cut-off on the reverser to compensate.

Arriving at Stratford-upon-Avon.
T DORRITY

After taking on water, the
tour is seen departing
Stratford-upon-Avon.
T DORRITY

We were given the ultimate accolade by the Rugby Station platform inspector. 'Who is in charge of this Puffing Billy?' enquired this worthy, again we guessed due to the Westinghouse pump emphasising our presence. Bill admitted liability. 'Will she run 'em?' came the request. Bill looked at me, I at him, we both looked to our new friends on the engine. We all smiled. Bill replied 'Why, is there a problem?' 'Yes, there is an express due through in 20 minutes, you either run 'em, wait, or go *via* the Northampton loop.' Now, no self-respecting engineman will normally decline such a challenge and we were not going to be the exception. 'No problem, we'll run 'em. Ring for the signal and we'll get going,' came the completely confident reply whereupon Bill ducked his head back into the cab, while the platform inspector hesitated to commit himself. He stood eyeing up our steadily panting locomotive for fully half a minute. You could sense his uncertainty. Suddenly he made up his mind, advised the signalman and almost immediately the signal came 'off'. In no time at all the last passengers were back in the train and we were away.

Arrangements had been made by the tour organisers, while we were servicing the engine, for unscheduled special stops to be made at Bletchley and Watford to help passengers get home. So it was Bletchley we had to reach, ahead of the express, travelling over ordinary double line most of the way. If we had expired there was no alternative route for the express to get round us, once it had passed Rugby. We could not let the side down, the honour of the Eastern Region was at stake. We were far from home deep in the heart of alien territory and on their principal main line, to rub it in, if we defaulted!

Did we go! Using the first valve she steamed a treat with a freshly cleaned fire. The stronger exhaust with a slightly longer cut-off did the trick beautifully. The firing was done 'according to the gospel', so much so that our Rugby man admitted enjoying firing 'little and often' as being more of a satisfying challenge. He kept the back bed thinner than the front and all was well. He was not too impressed with the long throw of ten feet or so to reach the front end of the firebox until he got the hang of it. As he said, 'we have a similar length on the 'Scots' but you roll it up there off the deeper rear section of the fire. You don't have to fire every shovelful the full length.' And did she steam! We held 170/175 lbs/sq in all the way. She was now running with the front end freedom for which a well-maintained B12 used to be so well known. Rugby was very impressed with the riding qualities; Stratford kept quiet and just smiled. She was a touch hard on the axleboxes but the big ends were not lumping at all and ran very well for an engine condemned for scrapping. I do not know, but

I will wager Bill Harvey had got to work on her when it was known she was to be purchased for preservation. Whether this was the case or not, 1572 certainly ran up the West Coast main line in a style truly reminiscent of former exploits on her native GE main lines. She topped 70mph as well – what a swan song it was turning into!

There are in existence a small number of ten inch [vinyl] records privately pressed through the good offices of a Mr Bob Todd. He it was who kindly sent me a copy as a special thank you and souvenir of the day's activities. I still treasure it as a reminder of a very unusual outing. On this record there are excellent recordings of parts of our progress onwards from Rugby. One track was made inside Kilsby Tunnel. To listen to 1572 as she went through this famous bore at just under 70mph is to listen to pure music! I can still recall it with no difficulty. I can visualise the reflected glare of the fire on the cab roof and tender front, plus the echo effect from the tunnel walls, as the four of us, not forgetting the star performer herself, enjoyed the moment. The Rugby crew really entered into the spirit of it. They had never seen, let alone handled a '1500'. She was so completely different from anything they were familiar with, and yet they were coaxing this excellent performance out of her as if they had run her for many a long day. Both men were following the advice we had offered and it was great fun to see it coming together so nicely. They were thoroughly enjoying themselves. Discounting the two station stops, we bettered the standard start from Rugby to pass Willesden express timings! We had 'run 'em' very successfully!

> **" 1572 certainly ran up the West Coast main line in a style truly reminiscent of former exploits on her native GE main lines. "**

All too soon our speed exploits were over as we slowed after Willesden to be diverted at Camden No. 2 box to regain the North London route we had left so long ago. It did not seem like the same day. We had covered a most interesting itinerary and though running well behind schedule, our passengers readily confirmed at Broad Street how satisfied they were with their day out and our efforts to make it so worthwhile.

We ran into Broad Street at 10.45pm, well over two hours late and well after the last normal service train had departed for the day. The 'powers that be' had kept the station open specially for us! As we came to a stand under that memorable glass roof, now sadly no more, the platform inspector could not resist asking us, as he consulted his watch, 'where the **** have you been – picking daisies?' Unfortunately our driver's reply has to be left to the imagination, it was one of the most colourful and apposite remarks I had heard in a long time!

After 16 hours continuously on the footplate, Bill Lockwood and myself decided we had had enough. But before taking our leave of the Rugby crew who had made 1572 talk to us in such a confident and competent manner it was necessary to describe to them how to put our dear old lady back to bed again. Bill was checking the driver knew how to use the Westinghouse brake, which steam cock controlled it and not to rely on it when leaving the engine unattended, such as on a turntable. Meanwhile I was explaining the drop grate mechanism to the fireman – where it was and how to work it. Throughout the discussions we were constantly interrupted by passengers who were keen to say 'thank you' and express their appreciation. It brought a warm glow to the heart as we later made our way down to the Tube to catch the last trains, just in time to get home.

As we walked from the platform the steady throb of the donkey pump reverberating around the otherwise silent station and echoing back off that enormous roof will forever remain in my mind. We both instinctively turned round to take a last look at our trusty steed who had performed so well throughout the day. I have not seen her since that day to this, although I have followed her subsequent journey into the ups and downs of her preservation story. Perhaps one day, who knows, I may yet step up into her cab. Whether or not I can still reach the front of her firebox with a good clean swing of the shovel might be a different story!

One little known fact that may be of interest, was the proposal to run a railtour out of Paddington, using 1572, some months later. Why it never materialised I do not know. I do know there was another telephone call to enquire if I would be prepared to repeat my performance in a similar capacity on Western Region metals. No prize for guessing the answer!

I would not like to even hazard a guess as to how many miles my footplate career gave me on the '1500s'. It would be a considerable total, but without any doubt whatsoever this day out with the 'Wandering 1500' railtour covered by far the most enjoyable miles of them all. Thank you 1572.

On shed at Willesden the day after the tour.
GEOFF RIXON

It is approaching 40 years since these exploits took place. Only in very recent months has the old lady once again been allowed out on a main running line. I understand she acquitted herself well during the 'Metropolitan 2000' annual steam gala weekend. I hope this is true.

Neither should we forget the man, who more than any other single person made it possible, the late Mr Bill Harvey, for his persistent refusal to send her to Stratford for scrapping. The old lady has had a chequered career in preservation, but nobody can deny the pleasure so many people get from seeing and hearing the only surviving British inside cylinder 4-6-0 in working order. I am pleased to have played a very small part in her ongoing story. She was a Southend engine for a very long while and I had several happy trips on her in the early 1950s. She has already spent more years in preservation than working for her one time owners – a very remarkable survivor. Long may her career continue.

The only drawback to my career was a very stiff back for a week afterwards. This would be gladly suffered again if the clock could be wound back to 1963 once more!

Ticket from the tour.
CHRIS BIRD

Tour postscript

BY DAVID BUTCHER

T he 'Wandering 1500' railtour article was originally written for the Great Eastern Railway Society *Journal*. It was later reproduced in the autumn 2003 issue of *Joint Line*, at the Society's request, to describe for members a unique event from 40 years earlier that had been arranged by the Society. By 2003 there were many members who had only heard of the trip with no direct knowledge of it. In retrospect today, the wider significance of what occurred can be better appreciated.

It is amazing to acknowledge that such a young Society – as it then was – could have even contemplated such an ambitious day out and that BR would permit a tour that relied entirely on an engine withdrawn two years previously for scrapping. This became the first such railtour in turn ever to be allowed by BR to operate over rarely used branch lines and on its main lines, using such a locomotive, and makes what was done – and so success-fully achieved – a most remarkable event for which both BR and the Society showed tremendous faith in the outcome.

In those days, nearly half a century ago, the occasional railtours always used either an engine still in regular traffic or a previously preserved and lovingly cared for machine taken temporarily out of its museum environment for a major overhaul before re-entering traffic. To have allowed a machine back into traffic for such a use with no major overhaul after being taken out of service so long beforehand was a unique event and without doubt paved the way for further such tours with previously withdrawn (but overhauled) engines to become possible, although this was not fully understood at the time. We knew we were achieving something different but not to the extent that has since emerged today, when steam railtours are taken for granted as being a normal sight on our national rail system.

Although no longer a steam engineman by 1963, I was able to contribute, by my presence on the footplate, towards the successful outcome on a most unusual 'unofficial day at work with a difference'. My regular BR employment as the yardmaster responsible for the large King's Cross goods yard could not be revealed for fear of possible reper-cussions. Apart from a very select few, my 'secret' remained unknown. This was because I could not exist officially as I was a working railway manager with no motive power responsibilities. For my presence on the day to have been formally organised could have

61572 makes an impressive sight as it passes through New Barnet on 5 October 1963.
THE LATE J MACHIN/ COLOUR-RAIL.COM

involved consulting with other departments and there was simply not enough time for that after it was agreed, literally on the day before, that my being available in the cab could be useful – and which, indeed, proved to be the case. I was thanked for my contribution by each of the crews involved – the Willesden men to Northampton, the Northampton men to Rugby and the Rugby men to London, plus the King's Cross pilotman Finsbury Park to Hitchin and the Bedford pilotman Hitchin to Northampton (who had travelled from Bedford *via* Cambridge to reach Hitchin). Only Inspector Bill Lockwood and the King's Cross pilotman knew my current background – the pilotman was personally known to me from firing to him in my past career and who tacitly kept quiet at my request. The inspector verified who I was before climbing on board at Willesden. He had received a telephone call at home the previous evening that someone familiar with the engine would be on board with the personal authority of Mr T C B Miller, the Motive Power Superintendent.

The other consideration came from the need not to broadcast my credentials. I decided that 'the least said the soonest mended' was by far the more sensible approach just in case subsequent queries might be raised. For example, maybe union sources might have complained had my official position been made known. By being 'economical with the truth', making no false claims and quietly blending into the background, I was simply assumed to be a motive power man from Stratford who was travelling on board, regularised by the presence of the official Stratford inspector. What interpretation the different crew members chose with which to satisfy themselves was never mentioned, questioned, or became any sort of issue. I looked the part in my normal work worn footplate overalls and footplate hat, serge jacket and meal bag (which included my obviously well used enamel tea can with tea/sugar brews to contribute to our refreshments) and simply was accepted as one of them. None doubted my 'authenticity' and a most interesting day was enjoyed by everybody as the trip progressed. No subsequent queries were ever raised, neither did I

LEFT: The letter from the Western Region of BR formalising David Butcher's presence on 61572 for a projected tour to Bristol. Note the letter was signed on behalf of one R H N Hardy.
DAVID BUTCHER

BELOW: The Willesden crew for the journey to Northampton from Broad Street and, on the right, inspector Bill Lockwood.
DAVID BUTCHER

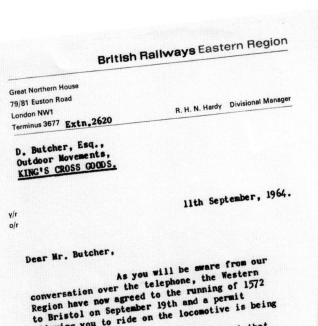

British Railways Eastern Region

Great Northern House
79/81 Euston Road
London NW1
Terminus 3677 Extn.2620

R. H. N. Hardy   Divisional Manager

D. Butcher, Esq.,
Outdoor Movements,
KING'S CROSS GOODS.

11th September, 1964.

y/r
o/r

Dear Mr. Butcher,

As you will be aware from our conversation over the telephone, the Western Region have now agreed to the running of 1572 to Bristol on September 19th and a permit allowing you to ride on the locomotive is being issued.

It has been pointed out that Old Oak Common men will be working this job and the Western Region have asked that you offer your help in a suitably discreet manner so as to avoid any upset.

Yours sincerely,
for R.H.N.HARDY
(Instructed)

61572 at Hitchin station.

ever mention 'back at base in my day job' what had transpired and nobody was ever any the wiser until 35 years later when I was eventually persuaded to write the subsequent article describing the day's events.

One can smile today at the simple subterfuge used by Bill Lockwood who, by being very 'economical with the truth', explained my presence as someone fully familiar with the engine, which of course was entirely true as were my vague references to having fired on her 'over a decade earlier' when she was a Southend engine!

It is remarkable to recall l did not see 1572 again until climbing aboard her 40 years later to the exact day, on 5 October 2003, at Weybourne shed as the invited guest of the Society. It brought back many memories and was as equally enjoyable for me as the original day out had been.

Long may 8572 continue to give pleasure to all who see her. The cost of periodic overhauls is very expensive and financial support is always needed. All donations, however small, can be made direct to the Society, which keeps them allocated separately for this purpose, and will be most gratefully received.